The Machinery of Your Body

Question:

I know I need food for energy and that any machine needs energy to make it run. Does this mean that I am just another machine like an automobile or an electric fan? I don't think I like this idea.

Let's start out by answering your question very directly. You are not *just* a machine. I don't know of any machine that could think up a question like yours. You must have been doing a lot of thinking, and no one has yet built a machine which really thinks. We have learned to make wonderful machines called computers which can solve long mathematical problems. However, the real thinking still is done by people who run the computers.

It is hard to imagine a machine which could write a poem or a story, or paint a picture, or love its mother, or want to worship God. It is my personal belief that no one will ever build a machine as wonderful as you are.

I think I have answered the real question you had in mind. You are not *just* a machine. You are something very much more.

Now I think you might wonder, "Am I a machine at all?" And the answer to this is, "Yes, you are." Maybe it will be easier if we say that your body is a machine. The human body, just like the body of a fish or a bird or a dog, is a piece of machinery. It has pumps and valves and cords and levers. It has all manner of fancy little gadgets built in. It even has a musical instrument. (If you can't sing, maybe you can whistle.) As you suggested in your question, it needs energy to make it run. And your body gets its energy from the food you eat.

Let's talk a little more about food, because it is more important to you than just to keep you from getting hungry. Food provides the materials which you need to keep your machinery in repair. And when you are growing up, food provides the stuff from which your body makes more machinery. But most of the food you eat is burned — yes, **burned,** in your body — even though very slowly. And the burning process provides the energy to keep you going.

In this matter of providing energy, food for your body is something like gasoline for an automobile. To keep a car running, you have to keep putting gasoline in the tank. And to keep your body going, you have to shovel in food (although it is better to eat politely).

Now that we have made the comparison between your body and an automobile, let's realize that there are also a lot of differences. I think there is one that is very interesting. When a car runs out of gas, how long can it keep running? Well, it may coast a little, but the motor stops right now. How long do you think your body could keep working if you stopped eating? Well, I'm not sure of an exact length of time (and I hope you're not silly enough to try), but the answer is that you could live much longer than you would think. You see, your body has its own stored-up reserves of food tucked away inside. And these could keep you going for a long time.

Some animals like the groundhog can live right through the winter with hardly a bite. Of course, this isn't quite fair because the groundhog has a special trick of **hibernating.** Somehow he can make his body run extra slowly while he is asleep during the long winter.

Even humans can do pretty well without the groundhog's trick. As near as I can find out, the record was set by an Irishman named Terence MacSwiney back in 1920. Terence got so mad that he vowed never to eat again. And he didn't. He went on a hunger strike for 74 days, and the only thing that stopped him was that he died. There is also a record of a scientist who went without food for as long as 50 days just to find out how his body would work during starvation. Of course he got weaker and weaker, the longer he went.

I hope I have answered your question. The real *you* is a lot more than *just* a machine. And yet your body does work much like a machine. It is a fine piece of machinery that you will have to live with all your life. It's a good idea to know as much as you can about it and take as good care of it as you can. You can't trade it in on a new one.

How Food Keeps You Going

Question:
I think I understand the idea that I need food to provide the energy to keep my body working. But what about this burning of food in my body? I thought that if anything burns there must be a fire.

You know, you are almost right. We do usually think that *burning* and *fire* go together. A fire gives off heat because something in it gets very hot. So, really, the important idea about burning is that it gives off heat. Actually, it is possible to make something burn so slowly that it cannot make heat fast enough to give a fire. You might not want to call this burning at all. So let's use a correct scientific term. Any burning, fast or slow, with or without a fire, can be called **combustion.**

In addition to giving off heat, combustion has two other characteristics. It requires **oxygen,** one of the gases in the air. And it usually produces another gas, **carbon dioxide.**

You can see some of these characteristics in an experiment with a burning candle. You need a candle about four inches long, a coffee can or a bowl, and an empty milk bottle or soda pop bottle. First we must attach the candle to the bottom of the coffee can or bowl. Light the candle and drop a little hot wax onto the bottom of the dry can. Then quickly press the base

of the candle into the little puddle of hot wax and hold it steady until the wax hardens. The candle is now standing straight up in the center of the can. Fill the can about a quarter-full of water and then light the candle. Hold the bottle upside down and lower it over the candle and down into the water and let it rest on the bottom of the can. The candle becomes sealed up inside the bottle.

Things happen pretty fast in this experiment, and you have to watch carefully. It is best to have someone like your father or mother to help. Notice that at first a little air bubbles out from the neck of the bottle because the candle flame heats the air in the bottle and makes it expand. Then water is sucked up rapidly into the bottle — even when the candle is

still burning. And then the candle stops burning.

If you try to repeat the experiment right away, things will happen differently. The candle will go out almost as soon as you put the bottle over it. Try it and see. It acts as if the gas in the bottle won't allow the candle to burn at all. So let's put some fresh air in the bottle. The surest way to do this is to fill the bottle with water to drive out the old air. Then pour out the water to let in fresh air. Now try the experiment again.

Back about the time of the American Revolution, famous scientists were doing just the same kind of experiment. What is the magic stuff in air that will allow combustion? And what happens to air when combustion takes place? It took the work of many people to solve the mystery. Each one got a little closer to the answer. Finally the French scientist, Lavoisier (la-vwa-z-yay) really figured it out correctly. He discovered that one of the gases in air **(oxygen)** is needed and used up by combustion. And another gas **(carbon dioxide)** is produced.

When a candle burns there is more oxygen taken out of the air than the carbon dioxide which is put back in. So there will be less air in the bottle when the candle has burned out. And once all the oxygen is gone, nothing will burn in the bottle.

Lavoisier wondered whether com-

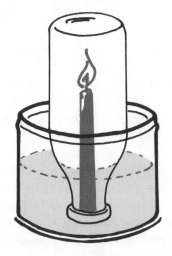
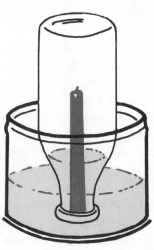

bustion also occurs in the body of an animal. It was known that after a candle burned out in a bottle, an animal couldn't live in that air, either. Or if an animal had been in a jar for some time, then a candle wouldn't burn in the jar at all. What an animal does to air, we call **respiration.**

Maybe respiration is just a special kind of combustion. Lavoisier proved that it is. He measured the amount of heat and the amount of carbon dioxide produced by a guinea pig in three hours. Then he measured the amount of carbon dioxide produced when a little piece of coal burned. Of course the piece of coal burned rapidly with a little fire and was all gone in a few minutes.

Lavoisier compared his measurements, and this is what he found. Whenever a quart of carbon dioxide was formed — either by the burning of coal or by the guinea pig — just about the same amount of heat was formed. Lavoisier was convinced. He said, "Respiration must be a combustion, very slow of course, but otherwise like the burning of coal."

In the 200 years since Lavoisier, his experiment has been done many times. It has been done on mice and on guinea pigs, on dogs and on people. Always the result is the same. All of us animals have a respiration which is very much like the combustion of a burning candle or a burning piece of coal. Respiration and combustion really are ways of releasing stored-up chemical energy. And that's how our bodies work. They are machines powered by chemical energy stored up in the food we eat.

Of course, today, our instruments are better than Lavoisier's and our measurements are more exact. We can see that not all of the energy of respiration appears as heat right away. Some of it is stored up as fat in your body. Some of it is used to repair or build more of the machinery of your body. Some of it is used to make your muscles work — as when you hurry home to dinner to get some more of that food to keep you going. "Mother, please pass me some more of that tasty chemical energy."

How Fast Can You Work?

Question:
You told about how fast my body is spending energy. This was interesting. But I have been wondering about a question that I think is different. How fast can I do work?

You are right. You are wondering about a new question and you have stated it very well. Some people might have asked: "How much work can I do?" I think you understand that how *much* work you do depends partly on just how long you keep at it. You want to know how powerful your body is — *how fast* it can do work.

There is an important idea that any machine uses or spends energy faster than it can do work. An automobile engine actually spends energy of the gasoline it burns about four times faster than it puts out energy to drive your car. And the same idea applies to the machinery of your body. It spends energy at about 2,500 Calories per day but it can't do work nearly that fast except for very short periods.

The rate of doing work is called **power.** And our most common measure of power is a unit called the **horsepower,** usually abbreviated H.P. It was invented by a scientist, James Watt, who also invented the steam engine. He wanted to measure how powerful his steam engine was as compared to a horse. Actually, since not all horses are equally powerful, we use a much better definition. When a machine lifts 550 pounds up one foot in one second, it is doing work at the rate of one horsepower (1 H.P.).

Most of our motors and engines are rated in horsepower. The electric motor in a washing machine is about ¼ H.P. The engines in little automobiles are about 50 H.P. and in big cars they may be more than 200 H.P. Some of the big diesel locomotives have 6,000 H.P.

How many horsepower does your body have? This is pretty hard to measure because your body does so many different jobs. For most jobs,

How Much Energy Do You Use Each Day?

Question:
How much energy does my body use in a day?

I like this question even though I had to do a lot of looking-up in books to find you the best answer I could. Here's an answer: Your body needs about 2,500 Calories per day. This is not a very exact answer and we will see why. But first let's get some idea of how much energy this is that you are spending every day.

In the illustration, you will see several common fuels and how much of each it would take to provide the 2,500 Calories which you need each day. Of course your body can't use coal or gasoline. I thought you might like to compare the fuels you can use — like sugar and butter — with the fuels which other machines use.

One trouble with just looking at amounts of fuels is that they don't seem like very much. They are really loaded with stored chemical energy. So let's make a different kind of comparison. If you could take the energy of any one of these amounts of fuels, and

Fuels Containing 2,500 Calories of Energy

gasoline	coal
1/2 pound	4/5 pound

not all of your muscles are working. And you know that if you are running very fast or working very hard, you can't keep it up all the time. So you will see why it is hard to get an answer to your question.

One answer to your question was obtained in a famous experiment by Professors Henderson and Haggard of Yale University. They were studying the Yale rowing crew of 1924 which set several records and then won their race at the Olympic games. In several races they rowed 1¼ miles in a little less than 6 minutes. The eight men of the crew were very fine athletes.

Professors Henderson and Haggard figured that rowing is the kind of exercise in which a person can do work fastest over a period of several minutes. In rowing, you use most of your muscles. When you pull at the oar with your arms, you also push back with your legs. So they wanted to know what horsepower the crew was really putting out. They loaded the eight men into their boat (actually it is called a racing shell) and gave them a joy ride. They pulled the shell with a motorboat at exactly the same speed

which the men had rowed. They found that it took just about 4 H.P. to make the shell go that fast. So they knew that, in rowing, the eight men were putting out 4 H.P. and that meant that for the six minutes of the race, each man was doing work at just about ½ H.P. So there's an answer.

Actually, for very short periods, a person can work even faster. But no one can keep it up. Not even a trained athlete can do work at ½ H.P. for very long. And most of us cannot do work nearly so fast. Most people, working steadily at some job all day, can't do work any faster than about 1/10 H.P. Perhaps this is the best answer.

Compared to the many engines and motors which do most of our work, your body doesn't seem so very powerful — and it isn't. We are fortunate to live in a world where we have machines to do most of the hard work. The wonderful thing about the human body is not its power. Think of how many different kinds of jobs it can do. And the next time you wave to the engineer of a locomotive, think of that big 6,000 H.P. locomotive being run by a puny 1/10 H.P. human.

somehow change it over perfectly and completely into mechanical energy, how much would it be? It would be enough to lift four automobiles to the top of the Washington Monument. I don't know why anyone would want to do this, but it does give you the idea. This 2,500 Calories you spend every day is a great deal of energy.

Now we should see why my answer could not be very exact. How much energy you spend each day is called your **metabolic rate.** It is a measure of how fast you are living. People differ a lot, don't they? And one of the ways in which they differ most is in what they do. For example, I know boys and girls who seem to be on the go all the time. It's even hard for them to sit still in school. I also know some who seem never to do a bit more than they have to. They even lie down to watch television. Since people differ so much in what they do and in how fast they spend energy, I can't tell you just exactly how fast YOU spend it. If you are lazy, you might spend only 2,000 Calories; or if you are really hustling, you might spend 3,000 Calories each day.

How can we measure your metabolic rate? Well, since you get the energy by combustion (or burning) of food, we could measure the exact amount of food you stow away each day. Actually, most of us eat just about as much food each day, and

burn it up, as is needed to provide the energy for our metabolic rate. If we eat too much food, we get fat because we just store up some of the extra energy as fat. And if we don't eat enough, we will get too thin.

A better way to measure your metabolic rate is to measure how much oxygen you need to burn your food. It turns out that every quart of oxygen that you use up in breathing means a release of 5 Calories of energy. So it is equally correct to say either that your metabolic rate is about 2,500 Calories per day or to say that it is about 500 quarts of oxygen per day. If we collect the air that you breathe out during some period of time and measure how much oxygen you took out of that air, then we can tell how fast you were spending energy.

I think there is another question you might like to know about. How fast can you spend energy for a short period if you try just as hard as you can? Well, of all the kinds of things you do, there is only one that really makes any big increase in your rate of spending energy. This is muscular exercise. If you go out and run as fast as you can, you will spend energy about 15 times as fast as you are spending it right now. (I assume you are now quietly reading and not bouncing up and down in your chair.)

I have used the term "spending" energy because I just couldn't think of a better word. I did not mean that energy is just like money. At least you don't have to worry about saving it. In fact, you can't save very much energy without getting fat. There is one way in which energy is like money. You can't keep on spending it faster than you get it. In the long run you have to balance your budget. You are the manager of your body. You are the one who tells it what to do. One of your jobs is to control your exercise and your eating so as to balance your energy budget.

sugar
1 1/3 pound

butter
3/4 pound

Why Eat Different Kinds of Food?

Question:
You have told us that food provides fuel for the machinery of our bodies. Why do we have to eat different kinds of foods? Why do my parents make me eat spinach and other vegetables? Wouldn't it be simpler to eat just one kind of food?

In the last three articles we were talking about your body as a machine. The important idea was that your body needs energy to keep it going. As you say, food provides the fuel which gives this energy. The answer to your question lies in a second idea: Your body also needs other materials to keep it running. Let's see why this is and what kinds of things your body needs.

It might be helpful if we think first of some other machine, like your automobile. It needs gasoline as its fuel. It needs a lot of other things, too. You have to check often to see that it has enough water in the battery and radiator, enough air in the tires, and enough oil in the engine. Sometimes parts of the machinery wear out and must be replaced or repaired.

Your body is an even more complicated machine than an automobile. And you can't just shut off the motor. In every living thing the machinery has to keep running. It is true that hospitals are a little like garages. Doctors with wonderful tools and skill can make some of the very serious repairs — such as setting a broken leg. But I think you see the important idea. Your body is designed to keep running for a long time. It's not only a machine, it must be a machine which can keep repairing itself as it goes.

Let's make a list of the kinds of things your body does need and think a little about why you need each of them.

The stuff you need the most is just plain **water.** You need almost two quarts each day, although a lot of that is hidden in the foods you eat. Why should you need so much? Well, just as all living machinery, yours has to be very wet to work. Most of you — about two-thirds — is water. In fact, if you get to feeling unkindly toward yourself someday, you might say that you are just a big old water bag. I know this sounds impossible. You might think that you ought to be oozing along the ground instead of walking straight and tall. Anyway, the idea right now is that a lot of you is water and that you are losing some of it all the time in sweat, in the air you breathe out, and mostly in your urine. So you have to keep putting water back in.

The foods that provide most of the fuel for energy are of two kinds. One is called **carbohydrate** (kar-bo-hi-drate). Carbohydrates include foods like sugar and fruits and honey, which you recognize because they are sweet, and starch, which isn't sweet at all. Potatoes, rice, and bread are starchy foods. Carbohydrates are fuels which your body burns easily and rapidly.

A second kind of fuel for your body is **fat.** Butter and margarine and the fats in milk and meat probably provide most of the fat in your diet. Fats are a little more difficult for your body to burn, but they are packed with a lot more energy than the carbohydrates. Whenever an animal eats more than it needs, whether carbohydrate or fat, it stores the extra energy in the form of fat. For wild animals this is important because sometimes they have to go a long time without food. For some of us humans who eat regularly — and sometimes too much — storing up fat is not so good.

Another kind of foodstuff that you need is **protein.** There is a lot of protein in meat and eggs and cheese. And there is at least some protein in many of our foods. Protein is mighty impor-

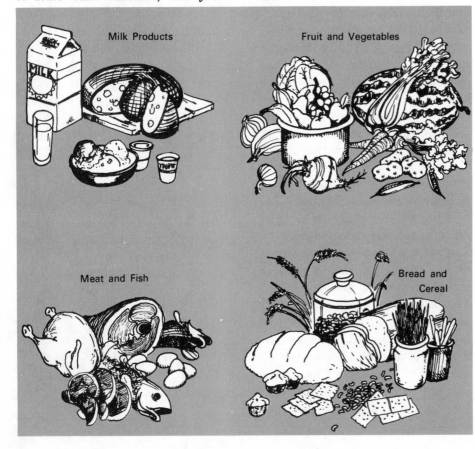

Milk Products

Fruit and Vegetables

Meat and Fish

Bread and Cereal

tant stuff because it is the real working machinery of all living things. Bit by bit the protein wears out and has to be replaced. Plants can build their own proteins from very simple materials, but animals can't. Animals must eat protein from plants or from other animals, and then rebuild or rearrange it to make their own special machinery. So, you see, you must keep eating protein just to keep your machinery in good repair.

You also have a need for **mineral salts,** but only in small amounts — less than an ounce each day. Plain old table salt is important. There is a lot of it in your blood and scattered around in your body. And you need tiny amounts of other salts, like calcium to build bone and iron to build hemoglobin, the red stuff of your blood. Most of your foods, especially vegetables, contain some salts.

There is still one more kind of stuff in foods that your body must have: **vitamins.** These are very special chemicals that do different kinds of jobs. Most of them provide special parts of your body machinery which have to be replaced. If you were to put out in the palm of your hand the pure vitamins that you need each day, you would hardly be able to see them. And yet without them, your body just won't work very well. There are a lot of different vitamins and some are found especially in certain foods: some in orange juice, some in green vegetables, some in cod-liver oil, some in liver and yeast.

I'm sure you see the answer to your question. There is no one food that contains all the things your body needs. You really need different kinds of foods to give you a balanced diet. There is no one who should be more concerned about keeping your machinery in good shape than you, yourself. You will depend upon it for a good long time. And you are the engineer who runs it.

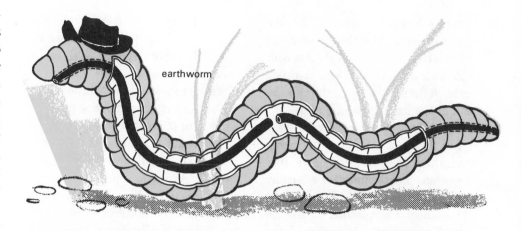

earthworm

What Happens to the Food You Eat?

Question:
You have told us that part of our food is used for energy and part of it is used to build our bodies. Some of the things I eat don't seem very good for building my body. I thought of this last night when I was eating a dill pickle. Does my body use all of the food I put inside? I guess maybe it doesn't use all of it, but how does it know what to use?

The idea of being made out of dill pickles does seem pretty silly (especially if you don't like dill pickles). I guess we eat a lot of things, not because they are valuable foods, but because they taste good. And some of us are not very choosy about what we eat.

In order to answer your question, we should first think about the way your body is designed. You have a body plan which I will call a tube-within-a-tube. All higher animals — dogs and rats and birds and snakes and frogs — have this same basic design. Even the little old earthworm, which doesn't even have a backbone, has this same design. The idea is that the outside of the animal body is really a tube with another smaller tube inside.

It is easy to see that the outside of an earthworm is built like a tube. It is not so easy to see that you are built like a tube. You have a lot of handles like arms and legs. But the main part of your body is hollow and, just like the outside of an earthworm, it is your outer tube. Your outer tube makes up most of you. It has your bones and most of your muscles. It is what you think of as your body. But for the food you eat, it is the inner tube which does the job.

The inner tube of the earthworm runs nice and straight from one end of it to the other. Your inner tube is not so straight. It has a lot of special parts along the way, as you will see on the next page. Food starts in the mouth and then goes down a narrow tube, the **esophagus** (e-sof-a-gus), to the **stomach.** The stomach serves as a tank or storehouse to hold food for a while so that you don't have to keep eating all the time. From the stomach, food goes through another tube, the **small intestine,** which is all coiled up and is about twenty feet long. Then comes a bigger but shorter tube, the **large intestine.** Anything that is left by this time isn't food at all. It is stuff you just couldn't use and is called feces. It leaves the body through the end of the inner tube, the **anus.**

So there is your inner tube, very much the same as it is in other higher animals. When you swallow something into the inner tube, it really isn't a part of you, is it? You might think about the question in another way. If you put your finger through the hole in a doughnut, you might say that your finger is in the doughnut. But certainly you would not say that your finger is a part of the doughnut. So when you eat a dill pickle it doesn't become a part of you — at least not right away.

Your inner tube has quite a job to do. The food you eat doesn't just drop through. It has to be moved or pumped along by the tube itself. Even your esophagus can do a pumping job. It is true that a drink of water usually drops right down to your stomach. But, if you want to, you can drink uphill. Try this for yourself.

Put a dish of water on the floor. Lie across a chair or stool so that you can get your mouth down to the water. See if you can drink the water. How can the water get uphill to your stomach? Your esophagus must do some kind of a pumping job. It has little rings of muscle built into the wall. The muscle rings tighten, one after another, squeezing the stuff in the tube and pushing it ahead. This is the way food is moved all along your inner tube.

A second job of your inner tube is to break the food down into very tiny pieces. First you chew your food into bits — at least you should. Then the muscles of your stomach mix and churn the food by contracting, first at one place and then at another. And then the muscles in the wall of the small intestine keep up the churning and mixing. In addition to all this me-

chanical working, your inner tube also does a chemical job of breaking up food. It makes special and really magical chemicals, the **enzymes.** These go to work like tiny little people with axes and chop the food particles down into still smaller particles.

The result of all this hard work is that in the small intestine food has been broken down into the tiniest possible particles. As you keep breaking any material down into smaller and smaller pieces, you end up with very tiny particles called **molecules.** These are far too small to see. Even a little grain of sugar is made up of more molecules than there are people on the earth. So, you see, molecules must be very tiny, indeed. And that is how tiny the food particles get to be down there in your intestine.

Is this finger in the doughnut?
Is it a part of the doughnut?

We say that your food has been digested. You would never be able to recognize a ham sandwich or a dill pickle.

There is still one more important job to do, for the tiny molecules of food material in your intestine are still not part of you. They are just there in your inner tube. Not all of them can be used by your body. How do you pick out the right kinds? There is a very delicate lining of the small intestine which does this job — and we don't know exactly how. It is mighty choosy. The molecules of goodies which the body can use are taken through the lining and out into small blood vessels in the wall of the small intestine. Now they are really a part of you. They are in the blood and can be pumped around to the rest of your body to be burned or to be put together to make machinery.

There are some kinds of molecules (kinds your body doesn't want) which can't get through the lining of the intestine. And there are some things in the food you eat which just can't be broken down by your enzymes into small enough molecules. These things are left in the feces and never do become a part of you.

So now you see how your feeding system works. You can help it by being a little careful about what you put in it.

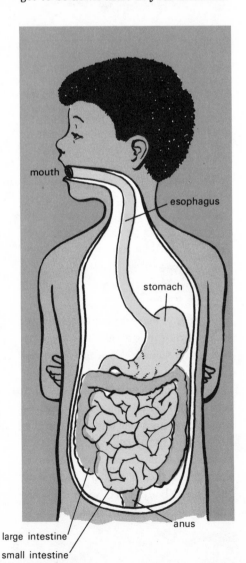

mouth

esophagus

stomach

large intestine
small intestine

anus

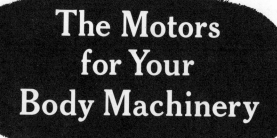

The Motors for Your Body Machinery

Question:
I have gotten used to the idea that my body is a kind of machine as you explained in some of your articles. But there are lots of things about it that you haven't explained. The machines I think about all have motors which make them go. I have been wondering where my motor is. My sister thinks it is my heart. I think it is my brain. Is either of us right?

I am surprised to realize that I had never thought about the question you ask. It is true that many machines do have some special part which serves as a motor. But for the machine that is your body, the answer to your question is: No, you don't have any special part which could be called a motor. The reason for this answer lies in an important idea about living things. Let's get the idea and then you will see the reason for the answer.

People have been curious about living things for a very long time. How do they work? Probably you have been curious about how some machine works. Have you ever taken apart an old clock to see how it was made? In just the same way, people began by cutting up dead animals to see how they were built. This led to a branch of science called **anatomy,** which is concerned with the parts of living things and how they are put together.

A great deal about animals was learned by studying their anatomy. I am sure it is no surprise to you that different animals have many of the same kinds of parts (or **organs**). Think of how many different animals have a liver and lungs and a heart and a brain. I'll bet it must have been quite a surprise to the first one who discovered this. It meant that the machinery really was pretty much alike, even in different animals. But the study of anatomy never did tell us just what makes the machinery work. There still was no answer to the question you asked: Where is the motor?

A very important event for biology happened just about 300 years ago. People were learning to make microscopes so that they could see things which are very, very small. One of the first people to use a microscope was an English scientist, Robert Hooke. He discovered that under his microscope a piece of cork looked as though it were built of many little hollow blocks, all glued together. He called each little hollow block a **cell** because it looked like one of the many small rooms or cells in a monastery.

Actually cork is just the old dead bark of a special kind of oak tree. But scientists looked further at thin slices of material cut from all kinds of living things. And wherever they looked there were cells. In living material, the cells were not just hollow — there was always something inside. In time they realized that the walls of the cells were not nearly so important as the stuff inside.

It took a lot of looking through microscopes — 170 years of it — but in time the idea broke through. All living things — elephants and humans and snails, oak trees and roses — are made of cells. And each cell, however tiny it may be, is a complete machine doing its special job.

Cells are not all alike. They differ in size. Some are as big as a hen's egg. In fact, an egg is a special, very large cell. And some cells are so small that they

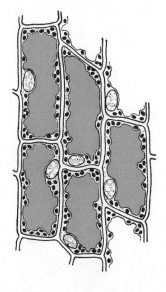

cells in a plant leaf

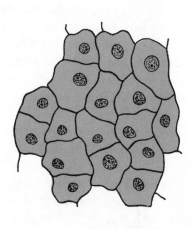

cells of the lining of your mouth

are hard to see, even with powerful microscopes. But most cells are pretty much the same size. An elephant is bigger than you, but not because it has bigger cells — it just has more of them.

Cells differ also in how they are shaped, in how they look inside, and in what they do. The cells in your brain do quite a different job from those in your liver or in the muscles of your arm.

And now here comes the especially important part of the idea. However different cells may be, there is one thing we can say about all of them. As long as they are alive, they are doing something; they are working. Each cell is its own little motor. It needs a supply of food and oxygen to keep it running. All of your many different kinds of cells must be happily working away in order that your whole body is working.

Now you see the answer to your question. You don't have any big special part that is a motor. You are made of billions and billions of little cells, each a separate little machine with its own motor. It is proper to think of your body as a machine. For your question, it might even be better to think of your body as an assembly of billions of little machines all working together.

There are a lot of questions about the working of your body which I have not explained. And there are a lot more which can't be explained because we just don't know the answers. If we knew how a living cell works, we would know a great deal about how your body works.

Today, scientists are learning how to take cells apart and study their pieces — just as the ancient Greeks and Romans began learning by taking animals apart. This is one of the exciting fields of biology. Scientists are asking the same question you asked but in a different way: Where is the cell's motor and how does it work?

Your Heart Is a Pumper

Question:
How does my heart work to pump blood?

Let's start by doing an experiment to see what it takes to make a pump work. We need two paper drinking straws, a glass of water, and another empty glass. We will use your mouth to do the work. Our problem is to pump the water from one glass into the other one. I am sure you can solve this problem with only one straw. All you have to do is to suck up a mouthful of water from one glass, as in Figure 1 (no fair swallowing any). Then squirt the water from your mouth through the straw into the empty glass. You are pumping water. All you had to do was to use your mouth and cheek muscles to make the chamber of your mouth get bigger and smaller.

Figure 1

Figure 2

Figure 3

Of course, in transferring the water, you had to move the straw back and forth from one glass to another. Most pumps, like the heart, are connected to two tubes so that they pump fluid from one tube into the other. Let's try two straws, one from each glass, going to the mouth. The trouble is that when you make the mouth chamber bigger, you just suck air from the empty glass. Even if there is an equal level of water in each glass, you just suck up water and squeeze water back into both glasses almost equally. We aren't getting anywhere in pumping water from one glass to another. We need some way to tell the water which way to go. We need some **valves.**

We can make a valve in a paper straw by pinching it flat for about half an inch at one end. Fix your straws as they are shown in Figure 2 and try again. Now I think that with a little practice you can pump water from one glass to the other, as in Figure 3. You can reverse the direction of pumping by reversing the straws. Do you see how the valves work? Water can move through one way but not the other. A valve is just a way of tricking the water so it can flow only in one direction.

Pumping water through straws seems like a hard way to get water from one glass to another. But the experiment does show you the two parts which we need to make the heart work. We need a chamber which can do the work by getting bigger and smaller. And we need valves so the blood will be pushed only in one direction.

Valves can be made in different ways. Maybe you have seen a door of your house slamming open and shut on a windy day. When the wind blows one way, it pushes the door open and rushes through. When the wind blows the other way, it pushes the door closed and the air is stopped. So even a door can be a kind of valve.

Now let's look at the illustration of the heart and see how it is built. Notice that it has two sides, right and left. The artist did not make a mistake in labeling the right and left sides. The heart is always drawn this way because we suppose that we are looking at it from the front side of your body.

The right side of your heart takes blood returning from all over your body through two large veins and pumps it to the lungs. The left side of your heart takes blood coming back from the lungs and does the much harder work of pumping it out to the rest of your body. Really, the heart has two entirely separate pumps built together so that they always work together.

Notice also that each side of the heart has two rooms or chambers. The two upper chambers, the **auricles,** serve as reservoirs to hold blood returning from the veins. The lower chambers are the **ventricles.** These are the main pumps — especially the left ventricle. Its thick wall is made up mostly of a very strong muscle which is the hardest-working part of the heart.

As a pumping chamber, the ventricle works a little differently than your mouth did in our experiment. It can't suck blood in; it can only squeeze blood out. Like all muscles, its wall is built out of many little cells which are like long, rubbery threads. The cells do their work by getting shorter, or contracting. When they contract, the whole ventricle wall squeezes together and pushes blood out. Then when the cells stop working, the muscle relaxes. Blood flows in and fills up the ventricle chamber. So the heart muscle works by contracting and then relaxing, time after time.

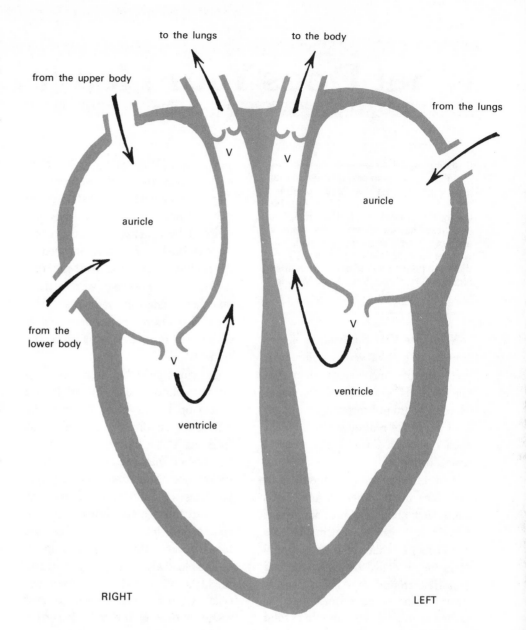

to the lungs

to the body

from the upper body

from the lungs

V

V

auricle

auricle

V

from the
lower body

V

ventricle

ventricle

RIGHT

LEFT

In the illustration you will see also the valves (V) of the heart. There are two on each side. Between each auricle and ventricle there is a big valve which acts as if it were made out of upside-down trapdoors. These are called the **auricular-ventricular valves.** Because this name is such a big mouthful, they are more often called the **A-V valves.** They allow blood to flow quickly from the auricles to the ventricles when the ventricles are relaxed. When the ventricles start to squeeze, the blood pushes against the A-V valves and closes them. The only way blood can get out is through the arteries. The second pair of valves in the arteries are called the **semilunar valves** because they are built of little flaps, each shaped like a half moon. They are pushed open and let blood out into the arteries when the ventricles contract. Just as in our experiment, the valves trick the blood so that it can move in only one direction, from veins to arteries.

You may think that all this sounds pretty complicated. And it is. But all these things that occur in the heart don't happen once in awhile. They happen every time your heart beats. And how often is that?

What Does Your Heart Do?

Question:
I think that a human or any other animal dies when its heart stops beating. So I always supposed that the heart must be the motor for my body. But you have told us that we have a separate little motor in each of the cells of our body. Now I wonder why the heart is so special. I think the heart is a kind of pump to push blood around through the body. Why is this so important?

Your idea that the heart is a very important part of your machinery is just so right. And you are right that the heart is a pump which makes blood flow around through your body. So I guess the real question is: What does the blood do and why must it keep flowing?

Your blood is pretty wonderful stuff and does many different jobs. Let's think first about its most important job. It is a carrier. Or maybe you would like to think of it as a supply train or a conveyor belt, carrying materials around your body. Each of your billions of cells must keep its motor running by burning food materials. Everything in your body (absolutely all of you) was made by your little cells, and all of the material which the cells used had to be delivered to them in the bloodstream.

The illustration shows you where the blood makes its pickups and deliveries. The whole job of the blood is to serve the cells, but we can show only a few of these in the illustration. And because the cells are so small, they must be greatly magnified to see any of them at all. The cells are supplied by a network of tiny tubes, the **capillaries.** Blood is pumped to the capillaries from the heart in larger tubes, the **arteries,** which have branches going all over the body. Blood flows from the capillaries back to the heart in another set of tubes, the **veins.**

Oxygen is picked up from the lungs by the blood. Food materials are picked up by the blood down in the wall of the small intestine. Of course these don't look like the food you eat. Remember that the food you eat is broken down (digested) into very tiny particles or molecules. These are strained through the lining of the intestine and into the blood. So the blood is like a thin syrup or soup.

The blood also must carry the waste products (or trash) away from the cells. Carbon dioxide, the biggest waste product of the cells, is carried back to the lungs. Other waste products are carried to your kidneys where they can be put into the urine and removed from your body.

In order to supply all of your cells, the blood must be kept flowing around the body. We say that the blood circulates, meaning that it flows in a kind of circle or circuit. In order to keep the blood flowing, the heart has to keep pumping. I think that is the answer to your question.

The blood and the heart and the whole system of tubes for circulating the blood are interesting and important parts of your machinery. I am sure that you have other questions about them. Right now you understand more about these than all the doctors in the world did when the Pilgrims landed at Plymouth Rock. They did not even realize then that the heart is a pump, and they did not know that the blood circulates or flows round and round. These important ideas were discovered by an English doctor, William Harvey, who published his discovery in 1628.

It seems strange that the science of medicine should have been studied for over 1,600 years before the basic idea of the circulation of blood was discovered. For hundreds of years scientists had studied anatomy by cutting up dead animals and examining their parts. They knew that animals had hearts. They knew that there were tubes leading from the left side of the heart. They called these **arteries** because, at first, they were believed to carry air.

They knew that there were other tubes, the **veins,** which connected to the right side of the heart. They realized that the heart beats or pulsates, but they thought that this was just a magical property of being alive. They supposed that the blood just churned back and forth between the veins and heart and gradually oozed out into the body. Later, they realized that there was blood rather than air in the arteries and left side of the heart. Then they supposed that

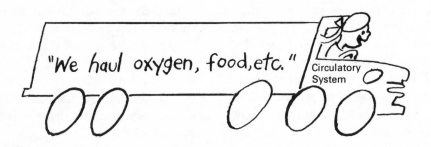

"We haul oxygen, food, etc."

Circulatory System

blood oozed through tiny pores in the wall between the right and left sides of the heart.

How did William Harvey make his discovery? He was a curious man and he did something new and daring. He opened up the chest cavity and watched the living, beating hearts in all kinds of animals. He watched the hearts of pigs and sheep and snakes and frogs. He saw that the heart wall was built of muscle and that each beat of the heart looked like a muscle at work. Every squeeze of the lower part of the heart was followed by a little bulging of the arteries. It looked as if the heart were pumping blood!

Most of us don't like to think of doing experiments on living animals — even when the animals are "put to sleep" by drugs so that they feel no pain. But without experiments on living animals we would know very little about how your body works. And William Harvey would never have made his discovery.

William Harvey also figured out how fast the heart pumped blood. He measured how much blood could be held by the large chamber of a sheep's heart — it was about three ounces. In an hour the heart beat more than 2,000 times. Even if only one ounce was squeezed out in each beat, the heart had to be pumping 2,000 ounces every hour. That is more weight of blood than the whole weight of the sheep. Where could so much blood be going? It could only mean that the heart had to be pumping the same blood over and over again.

Doctor Harvey wrote: "I began to think whether there might not be a motion of blood, as it were, in a circle. And I finally saw that the blood, forced by the action of the left side of the heart into the arteries, was distributed to the body at large . . . and that it then passed through the veins and so back to the heart."

That's how the discovery was made.

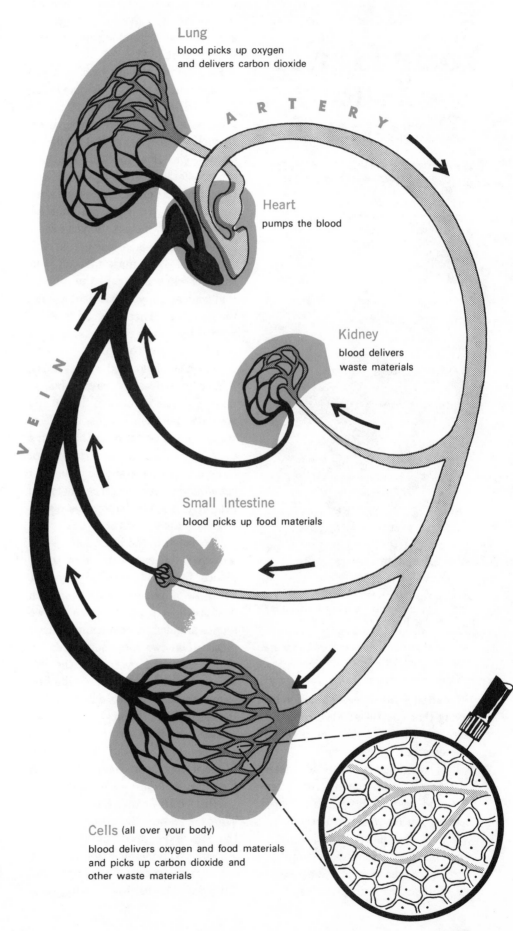

Lung
blood picks up oxygen and delivers carbon dioxide

ARTERY

Heart
pumps the blood

Kidney
blood delivers waste materials

VEIN

Small Intestine
blood picks up food materials

Cells (all over your body)
blood delivers oxygen and food materials and picks up carbon dioxide and other waste materials

Your Heart Is a Thumper

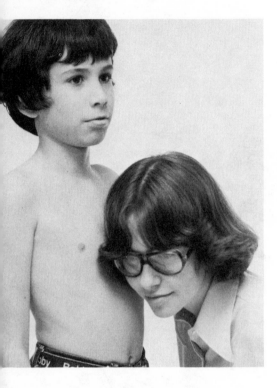

Question:
I looked up how fast my heart beats. It is supposed to beat about 72 times a minute. This is more than once every second. How can it keep working all the time? Doesn't it ever rest?

I started to answer your question by saying that your heart never stops to rest. But this is not really quite right. It is only part of the story.

It is true that your heart does keep beating minute after minute, day after day, and year after year. If it stops beating you have had it. Because, as you know, the billions of little cells in your body need a continuous supply of food and oxygen in order to keep working. Without the heart pumping blood

to them and keeping them supplied, they would just give up. We need to keep the heart pumping away. How can we let it rest?

By listening to your heartbeat you can learn more about it than anything I can tell you. Probably you have watched a doctor listen to your heart through a special gadget called a stethoscope. But you can hear the sounds of the heart by putting your ear against the chest. Unless you are a contortionist, you can't get your ear against your own chest. So you need a friend to help as a partner in this experiment. You must take off your shirts or blouses or pull them up so that you can get your ear right against the bare skin. Then you can listen to your friend's heartbeat and your friend can listen to yours.

Your heart is located almost in the middle of your chest cavity, but in most of us it is slanted to the left. So you must put your ear just a little to the left of the center of the chest. In a quiet room the heart sounds will not be hard to hear. You should move your ear around to find the place where you hear best. You will be impressed with how loud the sounds are.

Now listen to the heart sounds and see what you can learn from them. Notice first how regular they are. Then see if you can hear that each beat is a double sound. There are two sounds in quick succession and then a pause, then two more sounds and a pause, over and over. And the two sounds are different. Usually the first sound is softer and lasts a little longer; the second is short and sharp. The two sounds are often described by two syllables, *lubb* and *dup*. Listen again to see if your heart sounds this way: *lubb-dup — lubb-dup — lubb-dup.*

What causes the heart sounds? They are mostly the noises made by the valves or doors of the heart. Perhaps you remember that the heart has separate pumps on its right and left sides. The hardest working parts

of the heart are the lower chambers or **ventricles.** When the heavy muscle wall of the ventricles begins to squeeze, it forces blood against the big valves or trapdoors above and slams them shut. This is the *lubb* sound; it is longer and smoothed out because some of the noise also comes from the hard-working muscle itself. The second sound comes when the ventricle muscle wall quits work and relaxes. Then the blood out in the arteries rushes back against the small upper valves and snaps them shut. This is the sharper *dup* sound.

If you think about the causes of the heart sounds, you will realize that the ventricle muscle is working only during the first sound, the *lubb*. During the second sound, the *dup* and the following pause, the muscle is not working at all. It is soft and relaxed. If you listen again you will notice that the first or *lubb* sounds take up less than half the total time. The time schedule for your ventricle muscle might be estimated about this way: 3/10 second working and contracting, 5/10 second relaxing and resting.

You see the answer to your question. The heart does rest — and more than half of the time. It catches a little rest between each beat!

Now that you have heard the heart thumping away, let's do a little arithmetic about it. Suppose your heart does beat 72 times a minute. Can you figure out how many thousands of times it beats every day? Or here's a tougher problem: How many millions of times has it beat since you were born?

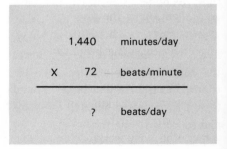

	1,440	minutes/day
X	72	beats/minute
	?	beats/day

How Fast Does Your Heart Beat?

Question:
You told us how to listen to the heart. I listened to my father's heart and he listened to mine. Then we decided to count how many times our hearts beat every minute. My father's heart beat only about 68 times a minute, but mine beat 90 times a minute. You said that the heart is supposed to beat 72 times a minute. I don't believe this, because we counted carefully and repeated our counts several times. Something must be wrong. Do all hearts beat at the same rate?

The answer to your question is: No, all hearts do not beat at the same rate. Whenever you can make your own careful observation or measurement, I think you should believe it, even if the books say something else. If scientists just believed what is written in books, they would never discover anything new.

I should apologize for giving you a number like 72. You will find this given in many books, but it is intended only as an approximate number for the heart rate or the beats per minute of the human heart. It is supposed to be the most likely heart rate for a young man when he is sitting down and his body is at rest.

Actually, your own heart rate varies a great deal, depending on what you are doing. It may speed up to 120, or even more, beats per minute when you are doing exercise such as riding a bicycle. If we want to compare the heart rates in different people or in different kinds of animals, we should have them doing the same things. In order to make such comparisons, we always measure the heart rate when the body is at rest.

Very often we can learn much by studying different kinds of animals and by comparing the ways in which a part of the body works. Think about the heart rates of the animals shown in the illustration. You may observe here this general rule: The smaller an animal, the more rapid its heart rate.

After comparing different animals, it will not seem surprising to you that your heart rate has been changing as you have been growing up. When you were a brand-new baby, it probably was about 140 beats a minute. You say that now your heart beats about 90 times a minute. This is common when you are about ten years old. In another ten years, when you are full-grown, your heart may be beating about 70 times a minute.

Now, all these numbers which I have given you are really only rough estimates. Even among healthy people of the same age, the heart rates are not exactly the same. For example, my heart beats only about 60 times a minute when I am resting. There are many other men of my age and weight whose heart rates are 80 or more beats per minute.

The body machinery in different people is similar but never exactly alike. This fact is important because it helps us to understand and appreciate each other. Wouldn't it be a sorry world if all of us were exactly the same, liked exactly the same things, and could do everything equally well?

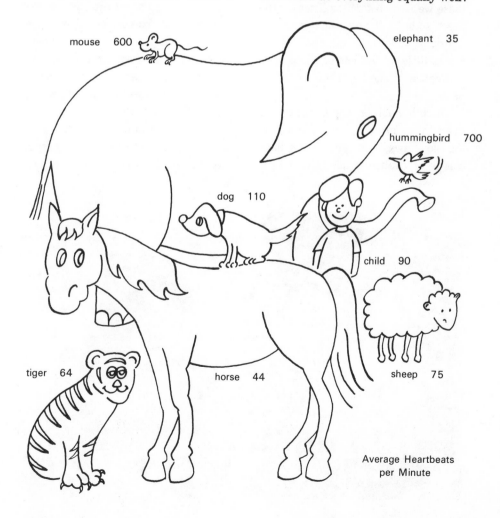

mouse 600

elephant 35

hummingbird 700

dog 110

child 90

tiger 64

horse 44

sheep 75

Average Heartbeats
per Minute

Automatic Control of Your Heart

Question:

I don't understand how my heart can beat so regularly. I must have some kind of clock. Is this right? How does the clock work? Where is it in my body? And if my heart beats faster when I am working hard, how does it know how fast to beat?

You have asked a lot of questions all at once. Really you want to know how your heart is controlled. Let's start out by doing an experiment so that we can see what the control system must do.

There are two simple ways to tell how fast the heart is beating. One of these we used before, to listen to the heart sounds. If you place your ear tightly against someone else's chest, just a little to the left of the center, you can hear the heart and count its beats.

There is another way to time your heart. Your arteries, the tubes carrying blood away from your heart, have elastic or rubbery walls. Every time your heart beats, it whooshes blood into the arteries and makes them swell or bulge out. And the bulge rapidly travels down through the walls of all your arteries. This is called the **pulse.** There is a place on your wrist where an artery is so close to the surface that you can feel the pulse.

Place your left hand on a table with the palm facing up. Now use the fingers of your right hand to find the artery, as in the illustration. You will find it over toward the left side, and you will know when you have found it because of its gentle throbbing. Each throb of the pulse counts out one beat of your heart. You can count your own heartbeat. If you want to make sure that each pulse beat corresponds to a heartbeat, you can listen to someone else's heart and feel his or her pulse at the same time.

Now find a watch or clock with a second hand, and you are ready for an experiment. First sit down or lie down and count the beats of your pulse for one minute. (Or you can count them for 30 seconds and multiply by 2.) Notice how regular your heartbeat is. You should repeat your count several times to make sure you are getting about the same number each time. Write it down.

Now stand up and time your pulse again. In order just to stand up straight, some of your muscles have to be working. And in most people this causes a small increase in heart rate. Now let's get some real exercise. Hop up and down on one foot 25 times and then on the other foot 25 times. Then sit down and immediately start timing your pulse again. I'll bet it really did speed up this time as a result of your exercise. If you wait another five minutes, it will slow down again so that it is almost the same as it was at the beginning.

What makes the heart so regular? Where is its clock? Scientists have done all kinds of difficult experiments on the living heart. But the simplest experiment answers our question. The heart of a frog or a turtle can be cut out of the body entirely and put in a dish of water with the proper salts added to make it something like blood. All by itself, the heart will keep beating away, sometimes even for an hour or more. We cannot escape this important conclusion: There must be some kind of clock or timer built right into the heart itself.

Scientists even know where the timer is in the heart. It is just a little clump of cells called the **S-A node,** located in the upper right part of the heart. These cells don't look very much different from those around

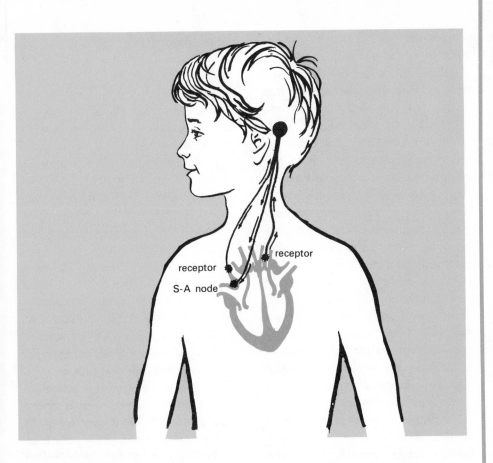

receptor

receptor

S-A node

them, and we still do not know exactly how they do their timing job.

Somehow there must be a way to make the clock go faster or slower so as to change the rate of the heartbeat. How is it done? For this you have one of the automatic controls of the nervous system. Located near the heart there are special **receptors.** A receptor is any gadget which can sense or feel and send a message. For automatic control of temperature in your home you may have a **thermostat.** It is a receptor which senses temperature. When the room gets too cold, the thermostat sends an electrical message to the furnace to turn up the heat.

The receptors for your heart control respond to the pressure of the blood. Some are located in the walls of the large arteries near the heart. Others are in the walls of the large veins. They send "slow-down" or "speed-up" messages over circuits of nerve fibers which go up to the back part of your brain and from there to the S-A node

of the heart. Somehow the clock is adjusted to make the heart beat slower or faster and to pump blood just fast enough for the needs of your body.

The control of your heart is a wonderful and automatic system. Even though it uses nerve circuits going through your brain, you can't make your brain alone control your heart. You can't say, "Speed up, heart." That isn't quite right. I guess you can say it or think it, but the heart just won't obey. Try it and see if yours will.

You may be a little peeved to realize that the heart is a part of your body which you can't control just by thinking about it. But really it is better this way. If you could control your heart by thinking, you might make a mistake. And personally, I'm glad I don't have to worry about whether my heart is beating fast enough. I'm happy to have the reliable clock and automatic control always working.

Your Blood Is a Carrier

Question:
You have said that everything my body makes and everything it uses must be carried in the blood to the little cells which do the work. How can my blood carry so much?

Your blood certainly does a wonderful job of carrying things around in your body. In order to answer your question, it will help if we ask some other questions. How much blood do you have? What is it made of? How fast does it travel?

Some people don't like to talk about blood — as if it were a nasty word. And some people don't even like to think about it. Maybe this is because most of us see blood only when we are hurt by a cut or a wound, and we think of blood as being ugly.

I would like to convince you that your blood is really clean and pure and actually is very pretty. How much do you have? In most people the blood makes up about 1/12 of the weight of the body. If you weigh 72 pounds, you have about 6 pounds of blood. That would be just about enough to fill three quart milk bottles. You may not like the idea of blood sitting in front of you in milk bottles. But try imagining it anyway. The red blood in those bottles would be cleaner and purer and prettier than any three quarts of milk you will ever see.

What Your Blood Carries Each Day in Pounds of Different Materials	
Water	4
Food Materials	1
Oxygen	1 2/3
Carbon Dioxide	2
Other Waste Products	1/6

Let's think about what your blood does have to carry each day on its many trips around the body. These things are listed in the table.

If you add up the amounts, you will see that your 6 pounds of blood actually carry almost 9 pounds of stuff every day. How can this be? It just means that much of the material in the blood is changing all the time.

Think about *water*. Usually you take in about 4 pounds of water every day. Some of this you drink. The rest comes in wet foods you eat. Most of it is picked up by the blood from your intestine. You also lose just about the same amount of water each day. It is made into urine by your kidneys, into sweat by your skin, and into water vapor by your lungs. And your kidneys and skin and lungs get this water from the blood.

Suppose you drink an extra glass of water. This extra water is rapidly taken into the blood. But the amount of water in the blood hardly changes at all. Your kidneys just make urine faster to get rid of the extra water.

Other things in the blood are managed in much the same way. Even though they are being put in and taken out all the time, the amounts of different materials in the blood are kept very constant. So all of the millions of little cells in your body are comfortable and happy with a constant supply of the things they need.

Of course, most of the stuff in the blood is water. Most of the other materials listed in the table — *food materials, carbon dioxide,* and *other waste products* — are easy to carry. They dissolve easily in water, just as a spoonful of salt dissolves and disappears when you stir it into a glass of water. They are carried in the blood all nicely dissolved to make a thin soup called the **plasma.**

Carrying *oxygen* is a special problem. Not very much oxygen will dissolve in water, and your cells need a big supply of it. Your blood could never carry enough oxygen just dissolved in water like the materials of the plasma. It needs a special way to load up with oxygen.

Carried around in the plasma there are millions and millions of tiny cells. They are called **red blood cells** or an even fancier name, the **erythrocytes** (eh-RITH-ro-sites). Every person's blood contains just about 15,000,000,000,000 of them, so you can see that they must be very small indeed. Under a microscope they look like little coins which have been pinched in at the center. The most noticeable thing about the red blood cells is that they are red. Because of them, the blood is red. The stuff that makes them red is what we want to talk about because it carries oxygen. It is called **hemoglobin** (HEE-mo-GLO-bin). It is a very special chemical.

Hemoglobin combines with oxygen very greedily. When it does this in the lungs, the blood changes in color from a dull red to a bright scarlet. So the color of blood tells how much oxygen it holds. Of course, many chemicals can combine with oxygen. The magic about hemoglobin is that it also is happy to uncombine and give off oxygen to the cells in the body where oxygen is being used up. So hemoglobin is a wonderful carrier for oxygen. Every time your three quarts of blood have been pumped around the body, its hemoglobin has picked up almost a cupful of oxygen and delivered the oxygen to your working cells.

You see that the blood is a good carrier. It is like a very large truck which can carry big loads of the materials which must be moved. It is also like a very speedy truck. Even when your body is at rest, your three quarts of blood get pumped around the body about once a minute. And during exercise the blood is pumped still faster. This means that for each of the materials carried, there are more than 1,440 big pickups and deliveries every day. I think that is very good service.

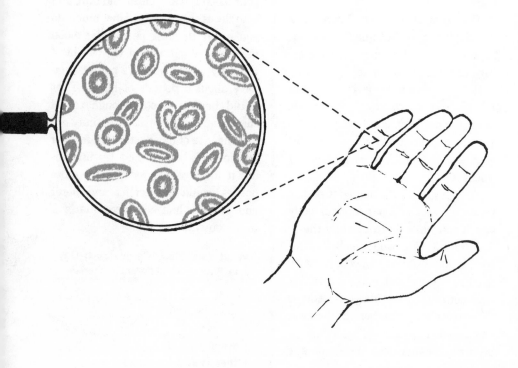

What Keeps Your Blood Pure?

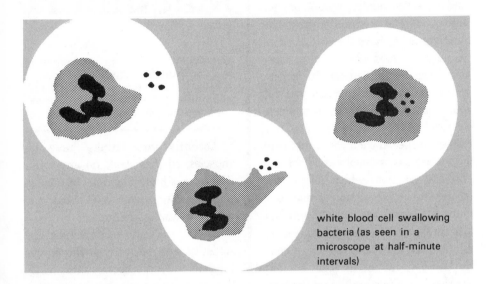

white blood cell swallowing bacteria (as seen in a microscope at half-minute intervals)

Question:
You have said that my blood is pure and clean and pretty. I don't think it looks very pretty. I cut my thumb yesterday, and it has a messy old scab on it. And how do you know that my blood is so clean and pure?

I must admit that a scab over a cut is not very pretty. But I have no doubt about your blood being clean and pure. If it were not, you would be mighty sick. Let me tell you why I can be so sure.

In talking about what the blood is made of, we found that it contains all of the food materials for cells of your body. The liquid part of your blood, the **plasma,** is like a thin soup.

You know that most foods will spoil unless we take special care of them. Some foods we keep cold in a refrigerator, others we keep in cans, still others we eat only when they are fresh. Why do foods spoil? I think you know the answer to this, too. In soil and water, and even in the air, there are very tiny living things such as **bacteria.** Some of these cause disease, but most of them just want to live

quietly by themselves. Some bacteria use special kinds of foods, but many of them use for food the same things that we do.

If we leave a bowl of milk or soup out in the open, it will begin to spoil after a few days. It may turn sour. Probably it will smell bad. When we say that food spoils, we mean that bacteria are living on it and changing it into their waste materials. Would blood spoil if we left it out in an open bottle? In time it most surely would. In fact, there are very few things better than blood for growing bacteria.

Now I think you see the idea. The blood right in your body, all nice and warm, would be a happy home for bacteria. But the blood in your body doesn't spoil. So it can't have any bacteria in it. That is how I know that it must be clean and pure.

You may be thinking about a new question. How do you keep bacteria from growing in your blood? There are many ways which the body uses. Let's think about the most important ones. First, your body partly seals them out.

Most bacteria cannot get through the tough covering of your skin. Of course you have some openings, like the mouth and nose, with no skin inside. And there is also the problem of accidents and cuts or breaks in the skin.

When you cut your thumb, what kept bacteria from sneaking in? Well, actually, a few bacteria probably did get into the cut. Then a special protective system went into operation.

Floating in the plasma and carried around in your blood there are several different kinds of cells. We have talked before about the **red blood cells** which carry oxygen. There is also another kind, the **white blood cells.** There are not so many of these. They have no color and are not so pretty, but they are very important. Some of them are the soldier or police cells of your blood. They gobble up any little particles like bacteria. When you cut your thumb, thousands of white blood cells clustered around the cut, as if by magic. And they were gobbling up bacteria as fast as they could. The white blood cells are always on the job, guarding against bacteria which would like to grow in your blood.

Now let's think about the scab

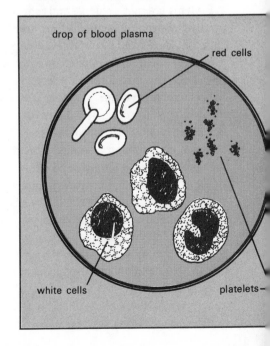

drop of blood plasma

red cells

white cells

platelets

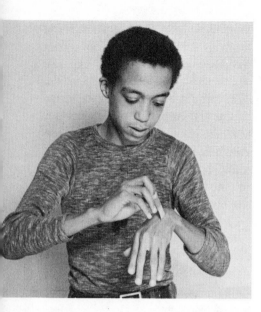

which formed over the cut in your thumb. If it had not formed, you would have been in trouble. You don't want to lose your blood. If you get a cut, you need some way to dam up the leak. Your blood has a very tricky way of making a scab just to do that job.

The liquid part of your blood, the plasma, has in it some special proteins. These are not food materials for the cells of your body. They are a working part of your blood. One of them is a very special protein, called **fibrinogen** (fi-BRIN-o-jen). It is the stuff which can make a scab.

Proteins are made of large and complicated molecules. Actually they are long threads. But in most proteins the threads are all folded or coiled up into tiny balls. In this form the protein easily dissolves in water. This is true of the white of egg which contains an almost pure protein plus some water. Suppose we boil or fry an egg. Then the egg white gets all tough and solid. Or suppose we bake a mixture of milk and eggs. Then the liquid turns into a solid custard. By heating proteins, we make their molecules uncoil to give threads which tangle together. We say that the heat can make a protein **clot** or **coagulate.**

Now maybe you can see the idea of how your blood clots to form a scab.

But it does not need heat to do this. It uses a chemical method to make its fibrinogen protein unfold into threads and clot.

Besides the red blood cells and white blood cells, there is still a third kind of particle floating around in your blood. These particles are the **platelets.** They have the special job of telling your blood when to clot. They have rough edges and tend to collect on any rough surface. When you cut your thumb, thousands of platelets collected on the sides of the cut. They released a special chemical. From here on we are not sure about all of the chemical reactions which took place. In the end, these chemical reactions made the fibrinogen molecules unfold into tiny threads. This made the blood into a thick jelly with red blood cells trapped between the threads. The jelly dried to make a scab. And the leak was stopped up.

So don't turn up your nose at a messy old scab. Don't pick it off. Let it do its job until your thumb grows new cells to fill in the cut and make it like new. Be thankful for your platelets and fibrinogen which work together to make your blood clot. And be thankful for your white blood cells which keep your blood clean. You need all of them working at their special jobs to keep your machinery in working order.

Number of Blood Cells

We have talked about three kinds of special little cells in your blood. Here you can see about how many you have of each kind:

Red blood cells —	15,000,000,000,000
White blood cells —	20,000,000,000
Platelets —	900,000,000,000

Your Breathing Machinery

Question:
Will you explain how my lungs work in breathing? I can feel my chest get bigger and smaller as I breathe. Is this because my lungs push my chest in and out?

Actually your lungs have no muscles, so they can't do any work. The work of breathing must be done in a different way. Let's think about your whole breathing system.

Look at the cutaway drawing of the upper part of your body. It shows your lungs as two large, spongy sacks hanging inside your chest. Inside the lungs there are millions of little hollow spaces containing air. The hollow spaces are connected by little tubes to a large tube, the **trachea** (TRAY-kee-ah) or windpipe. And the trachea connects the lungs to the back of your nose and mouth. Around each of the little hollow air spaces in the lungs there are tiny tubes or **capillaries** carrying blood. Here the blood takes up oxygen from the air spaces and gives back carbon dioxide.

You can see in the illustration how air can get into and out of your lungs. We also need some kind of pump to make the air go in and out. Since the lungs have no muscles, they can't do any pumping themselves. Let's see how the pumping is done.

Your air pump has two parts. Put your hand over the lower part of your chest. You can feel your ribs moving out and upward a little every time you breathe in. This is done by muscles between the ribs. Then you can feel your chest getting smaller when you are breathing out. The other part of the pump you can't feel. It is the

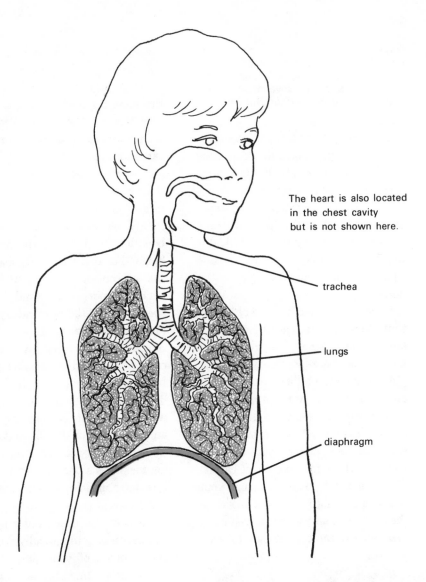

The heart is also located in the chest cavity but is not shown here.

trachea

lungs

diaphragm

do when sitting down. Notice how little air goes in and out. Probably it is less than a pint.

There also is an important volume of air which you can't breathe out, no matter how hard you try. You have an extra set of muscles which can make your chest get even smaller than usual. But the lungs are so spongy that you just cannot squeeze out all of the air. No matter how hard you try to breathe out, there will still be over a quart of air down in the little hollow spaces of your lungs. You see that in normal breathing each breath just trades a little of the air in the lungs for some new outside air.

Now you see how your breathing system works. The lungs are built so as to allow your blood to swap carbon dioxide for oxygen with air in the little air spaces. Then your chest and diaphragm muscles work like a pump to make you breathe and swap air in the lungs for new outside air.

In the course of a day you breathe in and out over 10,000 quarts of air. That is a lot of air and a lot of pumping for your breathing system to do.

CAUTION: Plastic bags are dangerous to a small child who might suffocate if one gets against his mouth and nose. Help to keep plastic bags away from small children.

diaphragm (DI-ah-fram) shown in the illustration. It is a sheet of muscle, shaped like an upside-down bowl. When the muscle cells of the diaphragm work and shorten, it is pulled tight so that it looks more like a plate than a bowl.

Your diaphragm and your chest muscles work together. When they are working, they make the chest cavity bigger. The lungs get bigger and the air pressure outside forces air down through the trachea to the lungs. Then your diaphragm and chest muscles stop working and relax. The walls of your chest squeeze the lungs, and air is forced back out.

You might like to know how much air you take in and push out each time you breathe. Of course this depends on

what your body is doing. First let's see how much it can possibly be. All you need is a plastic grocery bag. Gather the mouth of the bag together in your fist. Flatten the bag to get all the air out. Now take in just as big a breath as you can. Hold your nose closed and blow out all you can into the bag. You can see how much it is. You might even figure out a way to measure it. It will be about 1½ quarts of air. This is called your **vital capacity**. It measures how much air you can breathe in and out if you try hard.

Now let's see how much air you usually do breathe in and out. Sit down in a chair and get your plastic bag partly full of air. Hold your nose and breathe in and out of the bag. Try to breathe quietly just as you usually

21

How You Know When To Breathe

Question:
I once heard someone say that I could swim underwater longer if I took five deep breaths before I dove in. I tried this, and I think the idea is right. But why should this work?

The idea is right but you should be careful in trying it out. In order to see why, let's think about how your breathing system is controlled.

Your breathing system works to get oxygen down into the lungs where it can be picked up by the blood. And it works to get rid of the carbon dioxide which the blood has brought to the lungs.

I hope you remember a very important idea about the blood. The amounts of different materials in the blood must be kept steady and just right so that the billions of little cells of your body can work happily.

How can you keep the right amount of oxygen in the blood even though your cells keep taking it out? How can you keep the right amount of carbon dioxide in the blood even though your cells are putting it into the blood all the time? The answer is that you must breathe just rapidly enough to keep the right amount of oxygen and carbon dioxide in the air down in the lungs. Then the blood will always get the same big load of oxygen when it goes through the lungs. And it will always unload the same amount of carbon dioxide.

Now we must ask the next question: How does your body control its rate of breathing so that it will hold steady the amount of oxygen and carbon dioxide down in the air of the lungs? For this your body has a very special control point located in the back of your brain. And it has a special name, the **respiratory center** (pronounced re - SPIRE - a - toh - ree). Somehow it can "feel" the amount of oxygen and carbon dioxide in your blood. Actually it can "feel" carbon dioxide much better than oxygen. So we say that it is sensitive to the amount of carbon dioxide in the blood. Your respiratory center works by sending messages along the nerves to your breathing muscles, telling them how fast to work.

Most of the time your respiratory center works automatically. You don't spend much of your time thinking, "Now it's time to take another breath." Breathing is one thing you don't have to remember to do. But the rest of your brain CAN send special messages to the respiratory center. So, if you want to, you can decide to breathe faster or slower.

Let's try out your breathing system. Notice how fast you are breathing right now. Try not to change your breathing rate. Just leave it under automatic control. Probably you are breathing quietly and about 20 times each minute. Now try breathing any way you wish. You can breathe faster and more deeply if you try.

Let's try to fool your breathing system just a little. Breathe five times rapidly and as deeply as you can. Then notice that it is some time before you want to take another breath. Ac-

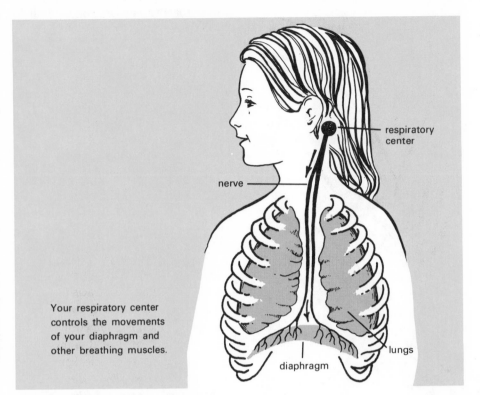

Your respiratory center controls the movements of your diaphragm and other breathing muscles.

respiratory center

nerve

diaphragm

lungs

tually you have "washed out" some of the carbon dioxide and increased the oxygen in the air down in your lungs. Your blood loses a little extra carbon dioxide. It takes a little while for the carbon dioxide to build up again. Un-

til it does, your respiratory center sends no messages to your breathing muscles. You just don't feel like breathing.

You can also do the opposite experiment. See how long you can hold your

breath. To make a fair test you must hold your nose besides closing your mouth. Maybe you can hold your breath for 20 seconds. Then your respiratory center can't stand the extra carbon dioxide which builds up in your lungs and in your blood. You feel that you just have to take a breath. Actually this won't hurt you. You can sweep away the extra carbon dioxide in a few deep breaths.

Now maybe you see the answer to your question. Try holding your breath again, but this time take five deep breaths before you start. This will allow you to start with your blood and lungs having a little extra amount of oxygen and a little smaller amount of carbon dioxide. I think you will be able to hold your breath longer.

Now that you know how you can hold your breath longer, please take a little advice. Your respiratory center works to protect you. You would be foolish to fool it too much. In managing the machinery of your body there is one important rule for everything you make it do: Don't overdo it!

See Your Heartbeat

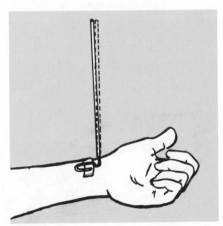

Bend a paper clip as shown, and slip a soda straw over the bent end. Then tape the paper clip to your wrist in the position shown.

Sit down and rest your arm on a table in order to keep it as steady as possible. If you have taped the paper clip in just the right place, the straw will move back and forth. It will twitch regularly, a little oftener than once a second. It is counting your heartbeat.

If the experiment does not work the first time, don't give up. Try putting the paper clip in different positions. Usually the best place is just below the thick part of your thumb as shown in the illustration. The paper clip must be held down tightly with tape. Or sometimes a rubber band slipped over your hand will hold it tighter and work better. Sometimes it will work better if the hand is bent backward over a milk bottle or a drinking glass.

If you have a watch you can time your heartbeat. How many times does the straw twitch in one minute?

How It Works

How can you count your heartbeat at, of all places, your wrist? Each time your heart pumps blood out into the **arteries** (little pipes) in your body, the walls of the arteries stretch. Most of your arteries are down deep inside, but in your wrist there is one close to the surface. It is so close that its stretching makes your skin move in and out slightly every time your heart beats. This is called your pulse.

The straw taped onto your arm is long so that a very slight tilting motion of the paper clip makes the end of the straw move enough to let you see your heartbeat clearly.

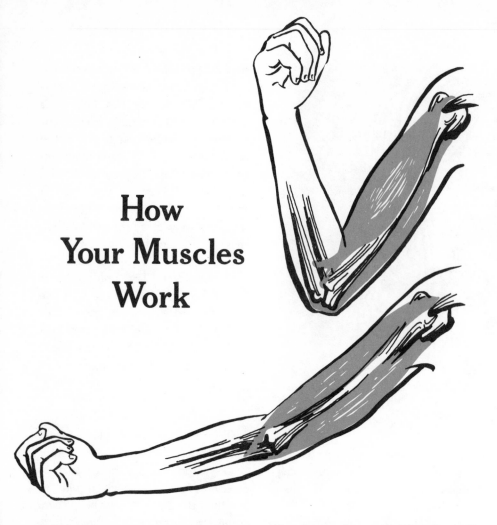

How Your Muscles Work

Question:
Can you tell me how my muscles work?

I can tell you some of the things we know about muscles and how they work. And you will see that there are some questions about muscles which we still cannot answer.

First you should know that your body has three different kinds of muscles. Your inside muscles, such as those in the wall of your stomach, work slowly and smoothly. Then there is the very special muscle in the wall of your heart which keeps working to pump blood. But you probably are thinking of a third kind, the muscles which move your arms and legs and fingers and toes. Because these muscles move the bones of your skeleton, we call them skeletal muscles. Let's talk about your skeletal muscles since we know most about them.

Any muscle can work only by getting shorter, by *contracting*. A muscle can pull, but it can't push. Since muscles work this way, they have to be arranged in your body in pairs.

Think about the muscles of the arm which are shown in the illustration. It takes a pair of muscles to bend your arm back and forth at the elbow.

If you move your right arm back and forth at the elbow, you can use your left hand to feel what your muscles are doing. First feel the muscle on top. It is called your **biceps.** Notice that as you bring your hand up toward your shoulder, your biceps gets hard and bulges out. Notice that as your arm goes down, your biceps gets soft and stretches out. Now do the same thing with the muscle underneath your arm. It is called your **triceps.** It works just the opposite of your biceps. If you make your arm just as straight as you can, you will feel both your biceps and your triceps get hard. The only time that both muscles

work together is when you try to hold your arm stiff and rigid. Try it and see.

Now you know something about the way in which muscles work — but not *how* they do it. This has been one of the important problems of biology. Many scientists have worked to find out what makes a muscle contract. Long ago they learned how to remove the largest muscle from the leg of a frog. They learned how to make it keep on working outside the body by giving it electric shocks.

Biochemists began to ask the question: What chemical changes occur in muscle as it contracts again and again? They discovered that muscle contains **glycogen,** sometimes called animal starch because it is much like cornstarch. As a muscle kept working, the glycogen slowly disappeared. Then they discovered that a new chemical, **lactic acid,** was produced. (Lactic acid is the same chemical which makes sour milk taste sour.) The amount of lactic acid formed was just about equal to the amount of glycogen which disappeared.

Biochemists decided that the chemical change of glycogen to lactic acid must be important in muscle contraction. But now there was a new problem. This chemical reaction

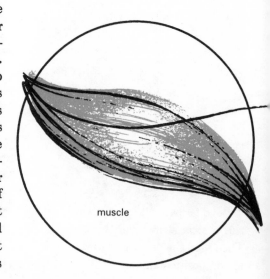

muscle

worked slowly, but a muscle can work very quickly. The contraction of a muscle is almost as fast as the explosion of a firecracker — but without the noise. Try bending your arm again and see how fast your muscle can work. Certainly there must be some very rapid chemical reaction.

Biochemists went to work to see what else happened when glycogen was broken down to lactic acid. They found that a new chemical was formed. When they learned what it was made of, they named it adenosine triphosphate. That's a pretty big name, but don't worry about how to say it. Just call it by its initials, ATP. That's what all biochemists do, anyway.

ATP turned out to be a wonderful chemical found in almost all living cells. In muscle cells it does a very special job. Muscle protein can be made into tiny threads. When ATP is added, the threads shorten very rapidly. It certainly does seem that ATP is the special chemical carrying energy to make the muscle contract.

Of course there is always another question: How is the muscle built so that ATP can make it shorten? Scientists have tried, every way they could think of, to see how the machinery of muscle is made. The diagram below shows you how its parts are put together. Let's think about how this was discovered.

Long ago scientists learned that they could take muscle apart to give two kinds of protein. One kind they called **actin.** The other they called **myosin.** They looked at very thin slices of muscle under microscopes which magnify about 1,000 times. It was easy to see that a biceps muscle was made of long, thin cells called muscle **fibers.** And each fiber was made of a bundle of threads which they called **fibrils.** Each fibril seemed to be marked by a regular pattern of light and dark bands. There must be even smaller parts making up the fibrils!

Scientists have learned to use the electron microscope which can magnify over 100,000 times. Under this microscope each little fibril can be seen as a bundle of still smaller threads called **filaments.** There are thick filaments made of myosin and thin filaments made only of actin. Each filament is only about 80 millionths of an inch long. The thick and thin filaments fit in between each other as in the diagram. Where they overlap there are dark bands. Where they do not overlap there are light bands. When a muscle contracts, the light bands get smaller.

So this is what we think happens in muscle contraction: The thin filaments of actin slide in between the thicker filaments of myosin. We have to stop here. Of course there is another question: What makes the filaments slide over each other? That's what scientists are working on right now.

Your muscle machinery has mighty small parts. It has filaments inside of fibrils inside of fibers. It would take over a million of the little filaments laid side by side to make a bundle as thick as one of your eyelashes!

Feel your biceps muscle again, and think what happens when you want to bend your arm. Your brain sends messages along a cable of little nerves to the thousands of muscle fibers. Then, whamo! In each of the many fibrils of each fiber, thousands of filaments go sliding over each other, somehow using the energy stored in ATP. Any one filament by itself couldn't lift a whisker. All working together, they give you a muscle with a mighty fine wallop!

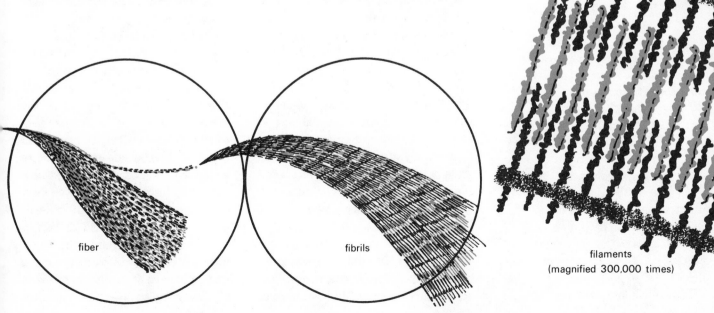

fiber

fibrils

filaments
(magnified 300,000 times)

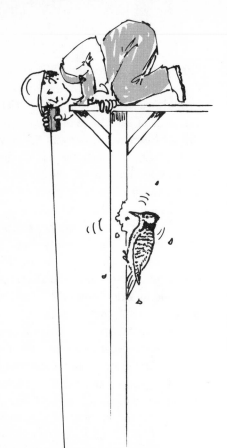

Carrying Messages

The Job of Your Nervous System

You certainly do have a wonderful control over your muscles. Let's see just how good it is. Let's try your muscle control. Hold out your hand in front of you with the fingers sticking straight out. Now see if you can close your hand, one finger at a time. First bend your thumb, now your first finger, now your second, now your third, and finally your little finger. If you try, you can bend one finger at a time. Some people can even bend the end joint of their first finger and keep the rest of the finger straight. I can't do this but maybe you can.

Bending your fingers one by one is just a way of seeing how well you can control your muscles. Somehow you must be able to send messages to each of the muscles to tell it when to work. The job of sending messages is done by your **nervous system.** This works in your body very much as a telephone system works for a city. Your nervous system is a lot smaller than a telephone system. It makes up less than 1/20 of all of your body machinery. But it is much more complicated. I can't tell you all about it — in fact, we don't know all about it. We can talk about the idea of how a message is carried.

Your nervous system is made up of billions of little cells. Each of these very special nerve cells is called a **neuron.** On the next page is a drawing of a neuron as it looks under a microscope. The most unusual part of it is its little thread or **nerve fiber.** This is only about 1/1,000 of an inch wide but it may be over two feet long. The job of the neuron is to carry messages along its nerve fiber.

Before we talk about how the neuron carries a message, we ought to think about what kind of a message it must carry. Some messages may be long and complex — like a letter or a telegram. Or suppose your mother says, "Janey, it is time to take your bath. And don't forget to wash off the dirt behind your ears which you missed last night." Really that is a complex message with several different ideas.

Some messages can be very simple. Suppose you are all ready to start a swimming race. You and your friends are lined up across one end of a swimming pool. You are crouched and ready to dive. Someone blows a whistle, and off you all go. The whistle was a message — and just about the simplest possible message.

The little muscle cells which make up your muscles are also ready to go. A very simple message can tell the muscle fiber to go to work. But how can the tiny thread of a nerve fiber carry even a simple message? This is your question. It is a question which puzzled scientists for years and years.

Almost two hundred years ago, it was discovered that a very small electric shock could start a message over a nerve fiber. Much later it was discovered that there are small electrical changes in a nerve fiber when it is carrying a message. But the more scientists learned about electricity, the more difficult it was to understand how the message was carried. Like other living cells, the nerve fiber does not carry electricity very well — not at all like a copper wire. And, in a nerve fiber, a message travels more slowly than electricity travels in a wire.

The nerve fiber really is built as a tiny tube. It was discovered that the inside and outside of the tube are electrically different when the nerve fiber is resting. The outside of the tube has a thin covering or membrane which acts as an insulator. There is an electrical difference of about 1/10 of a volt across the membrane. So the whole fiber is electrically charged up like a little battery. If we look at some one spot on a nerve fiber, what happens as a message goes by? The electrical

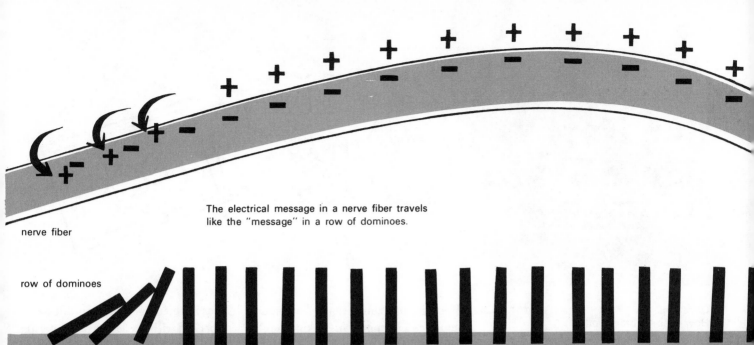

nerve fiber

The electrical message in a nerve fiber travels like the "message" in a row of dominoes.

row of dominoes

difference disappears. From very careful measurements like these, we have an idea of how the nerve fiber carries a message.

Here is what we think happens. Suppose we give an electric shock to some point on a nerve fiber. The shock travels only a little way along the fiber. Somehow it changes the membrane so that electric charges flow from outside to inside. Now the fiber is shocking itself! Again the shock travels a little way and changes the membrane farther along. In this way the shock keeps traveling right along the fiber. The little traveling shock is the message.

Even though the nerve message is electrical, it travels differently from electricity traveling in wire. It travels because the nerve fiber keeps working

to push it along. But the nerve fiber is very good at its job. The message can travel almost as fast as a revolver bullet.

If you play with a set of dominoes, you can send a message in a way which will show you something about how the nerve fiber works. First set one domino up on its end. Have a friend put a finger on the table close to the domino. He should close his eyes. If you push over the domino, it will fall against his finger and he can say something like "Yikes!" You sent him a message but you didn't send it very far. Now stand up a line of dominoes. You can fix them so that when one falls over it will knock down the next one, and that will knock down the next. If you set them up carefully, you now can send a message down the

whole line of dominoes to your friend at the end of the line. "Yikes!"

You may think that a row of dominoes is a clumsy way to send a message. It is. But it shows you the idea of how the nerve fiber works. A falling domino is like the electric shock that travels only a little way in the nerve fiber. And just like the nerve fiber, the dominoes must be working all down the line to keep the message going. There is one important difference. Setting up the line of dominoes again takes a long time. The nerve fiber is faster. It can get ready to carry another message in about 1/100 of a second.

A neuron with its nerve fiber is one of the most special cells of your body. It has just one job and it does it very well. It is a message carrier.

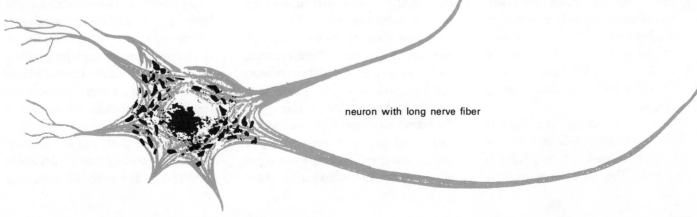

neuron with long nerve fiber

How Your Brain Works

Question:
How does my brain work?

This is just about the toughest question you could ask. It is difficult to answer because there is so much about the brain which we still do not know. It is also difficult because there is so much we do know. There are a few important ideas which everyone ought to have about the brain.

First, let's think about how important your brain is to you. There is no part of your body more important in making you different from other animals. There are other animals that are stronger or faster, or can see or hear better than you can. But you are smarter. You have a better brain.

It is also true that there is no part of you more important in making you different from other people. When you think about what you are and about what you hope to do in life, you are thinking with your brain — and mainly you are thinking about your brain.

Your brain is carefully protected inside a bony, round box which is your skull. You could say that your head is built like a turtle. Your brain, about a quart and a half in volume, is neatly packaged inside.

Your brain contains more than 10 billion nerve cells or neurons which are the special message-carrying cells of your body. The brain is a place where all kinds of connections between neurons can be made. In making connections, the brain. is like the telephone switchboard of a large city. It does its very complicated job in a very small space.

The drawing of the brain shows three main parts. The lowest part is called the **medulla.** It connects the brain to the **spinal cord** which runs down along your backbone. The medulla and spinal cord contain cables of the nerve fibers of neurons which carry messages between the brain and the lower part of your body. The medulla also has a number of little switchboards. These work automatically to control your heart and breathing and other parts of your inside machinery.

Back of the medulla is a second part of the brain, the **cerebellum.** It has a larger switchboard which helps to make the connections for messages going to your muscles. Somehow it keeps track of what your muscles are doing and helps to make their movements smooth instead of jerky.

Now we come to the very large upper part of the brain, the **cerebrum.** The most special part of the cerebrum is a gray outer layer. This is something like the rind on an orange. It is called the **cerebral cortex.** When you were a very small baby, the cerebral cortex kept growing and growing until it got all folded up and wrinkled. Its outer layer is about ¼ of an inch thick and is packed with the larger parts of little nerve cells. The inside of the cerebrum contains the many nerve fibers which seem to make all the possible connections between different parts of the cortex.

We still have not answered your question, but we have found where to look for an important part of the answer. What you want to know is how your cerebral cortex works. It is getting thousands of messages every second and sending out thousands more. It is really much more than a switchboard. It can make up and send messages, too. It is the control center for your body. It can remember and think. Your cerebrum is a busy place. How can it go about its business and not get all mixed up? Scientists have been asking this question for a very long time. Getting answers has not been easy. You wouldn't want someone poking into your brain, and no one else does, either.

Doctors have learned about the brain in two ways. They have done experiments on the brains of animals. And they have studied people who had wounds or damage to some part of the brain. From a great deal of study they have pieced together some important ideas.

Here is one kind of question which led to an important answer. Messages coming into the brain tell about the world around you. You have senses of seeing, hearing, touching, smelling, and tasting. When a message comes from the eye, how does the brain tell it apart from a message that comes from the ear? The messages by themselves are always exactly alike. So how does the brain know whether it is seeing or hearing? Finally the answer became clear. Nerve fibers from the eye are connected to the cerebral cortex at a special place. This occurs at the spot or area of the cortex marked with an **S** in the drawing. It is your brain's seeing department. Messages from the ear always end up in a different area marked with an **H**. This is your hearing department.

Scientists began to make maps of the cortex. Maybe they could find a special job for each little area. For many areas they were successful. Control of your muscles takes up a large area. What is more, each group of muscles has its own special part of the area. On the drawing, an **F** marks the place on the cortex from which you send messages to work the muscles of your fingers. And **E** is the spot for control of muscles to wiggle your ears.

When scientists had found the special areas for muscle control, and the special areas for each of the senses, the rest of the map-making got tougher. Most of the cortex of the human brain just could not be mapped. In many parts of the cortex, a wound does not cause any loss of sense or loss of muscle control.

These other areas come to be called **association** areas. They have connections of nerve fibers to the sense and muscle-control areas. Somehow we store up in the association areas our knowledge of the world around us. For instance, when you were very small you learned that fire is hot and can burn you. You put together or associated what you saw and what you felt.

The association areas of your cortex are the most wonderful part of your brain. We got so used to the things they can do that we just take them for granted. I want you to think about two examples which will show you what your association areas can do.

First I want you to think about memory. Look at the next line:
$$3 \times 6 = \underline{?}$$
You can fill in the blank. It may be so easy that you think I am silly. But I think it is pretty wonderful that you could do this. How did you do it? Somehow you had this information carefully stowed away in the association areas of your cortex.

Let's try one more. Suppose I make three pencil marks like this:

The pencil marks make a word, and the word gives you a picture. You know — it has four stander-uppers and two hooker-oners and two look-arounders and four hanger-downers and one swishy-washy. Of course it's a cowsy-wowsy. You may think that this is pretty silly, too. But I think it is really wonderful. I just wrote down three little pencil marks and I could give you a great big idea as a picture in your mind.

No one has been able to understand just how the association areas of the cerebral cortex do our thinking for us. But at least you now know a little about your brain. You ought to. You are spending a lot of time in school storing up bits of information and teaching your brain to use them in thinking. Here you have been wondering how your brain works — and it was your brain that was doing the wondering.

Brain (as seen from left)

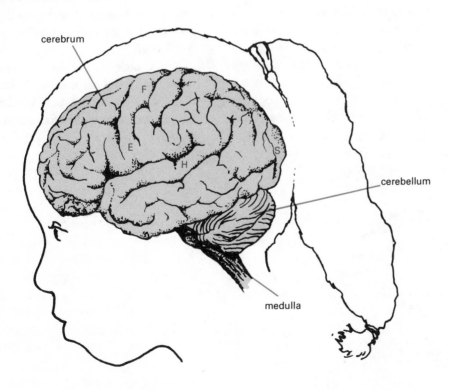

cerebrum

cerebellum

medulla

Simple Pathways for Messages – Reflexes

Question:
You have told me that I have billions of nerve cells which can carry messages. How do they get connected up so that the messages always go to the right places?

I think your question is just about the most interesting one you could ask about your nervous system. Let's think about how difficult the problem is. Sometimes, when I make a long distance telephone call, I wonder how all the connections are made between the right wires. Of all the millions of telephones in the country, how do I get connected to just the right one?

The problem of making connections between the nerve cells or neurons of the nervous system seems even more difficult. It must be done quickly and in a small space. Just like one telephone wire, one neuron of your nervous system never does anything all by itself. Neurons must be connected together to make a pathway for a message.

Most of the things we do need many neurons connected together to make very complicated pathways. Hitting a ball with a bat takes many neurons connected together to get the right pathways through the brain. When scientists try to learn about any difficult problem, they always search for some simple part of the problem to study first. Is there any simple pathway of neurons which will do something? Fortunately there is. The simplest and fastest kind of reaction your body can make is called a **reflex.** It uses a simple pathway of neurons which may not go through your brain at all.

There are many happenings which may cause your body to react in what we call a reflex. Suppose you are washing dishes and reach over to pick up a pan from the stove. But someone left the burner on and the pan is very hot. Your fingers let go and your arm jerks back. All this happens before you even have time to think, "The pan is hot." The nerve message reached your muscles before it could get to the brain. You acted without thinking. Your action was a reflex.

Suppose you are walking through the woods. Twigs and branches often slap you in the face. But they very seldom damage your eyes. By the time a branch hits your face, your eyes are closed. The muscles of your eyelids got the message and worked before you could think.

Reflex actions are almost always faster than thinking actions. Most of them work to protect us. We don't have to learn how to do a reflex action.

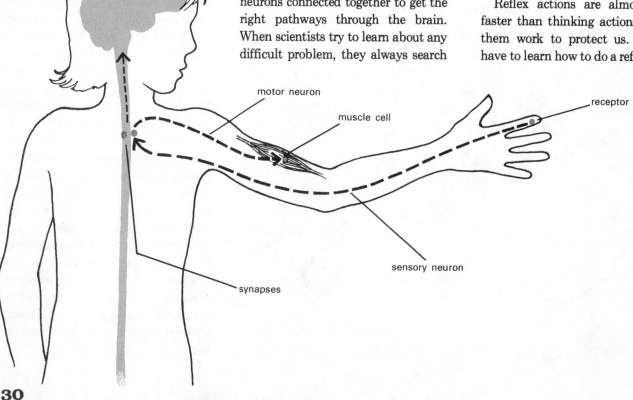

motor neuron

muscle cell

receptor

sensory neuron

synapses

It is built in. If something touches the palm of your hand, your fingers tend to close around it. A baby, just born and brand-new, does the same thing.

Some reflexes are actions which we could also do more slowly by thinking. If you want to, you can touch anything and pull your hand back. Or you can close an eyelid to wink at a boy or girl across the aisle. There are also some kinds of actions which are only reflexes. You can't make your heart beat faster or slower by thinking about it. It is controlled only by automatic reflexes.

Built into your nervous system are the simple pathways for reflexes. Let's see what parts are needed for a reflex action. Think about the reflex working to pull your hand away from a hot pan. We need two kinds of neurons. One kind we call a **sensory** neuron because it carries messages about the sense of touch from a receiving station or **receptor** in the skin of your fingers. The other kind we call a **motor** neuron because it is connected to one of the **muscle** cells in the muscles for your fingers and arm. One other part is needed. We must make connection between the sensory and motor neurons. For the reflex we are talking about, the connections are made in the spinal cord.

The diagram is really much too simple, but it shows you the parts that are needed. Actually, the many receptors and muscle cells and many neuron pathways between them **are** much alike and working at the same time. The diagram shows just one of the pathways.

The important new part we want to think about is the connection between neurons which is shown in the spinal cord. It is called a **synapse** (sin-APS). It is important because it is the part which must do the switching and connecting of neurons everywhere in the nervous system. Study of the simple pathway of a reflex gives us some important ideas about the working of a synapse.

First, it works only in one direction. The synapse shown in the diagram will pass a message from a sensory to a motor neuron — but not the other way. This gives a kind of traffic control. Secondly, it always takes a little time for the synapse to work. There is a little time delay in passing a message from one neuron to the next. This is why a thinking action takes longer than a reflex. Many more synapse connections must be made. Thirdly, the synapse is very sensitive. It is easily affected by chemicals like ether. Some of these chemicals, called anesthetics, are used to prevent pain and feeling during an operation.

Careful study of a synapse with a microscope shows that the endings of neurons come very close together, but they don't quite touch. How does a synapse work? We do not know all about it but here is one idea. When the endings of a nerve fiber get a message, they quickly let go a special chemical. The chemical oozes across the very tiny space in between and starts a message going again in the next neuron.

The ending of every nerve fiber has many tiny branches. It CAN pass its message along to many other neurons.

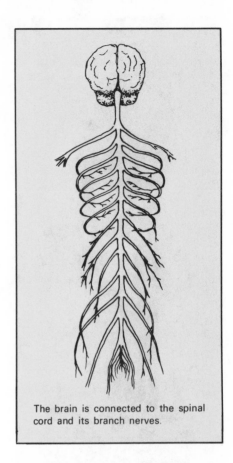

The brain is connected to the spinal cord and its branch nerves.

For example, the nerve fiber of the sensory neuron shown in the diagram always makes another synapse connection to a neuron running up to the brain. This is how you realized that the pan was hot. Still other connections can be made. For the billions of neurons in your body, the synapses are the switches which can connect them together. They work to get messages to the right places. In the brain, they somehow make the many connections which you use in thinking.

The more one nerve pathway works, the easier it is to make it work. It seems that any one synapse works better with practice. When you were learning to tie your shoelaces, you were pretty clumsy about it. Now, without even thinking much, you can tie them easily.

Now you know a little about how nerve messages get started and how they are switched over the right nerve pathways to speed around through your body.

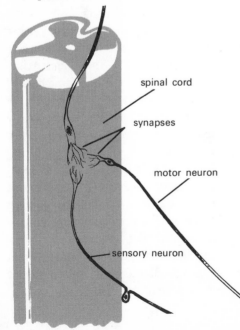

spinal cord

synapses

motor neuron

sensory neuron

How Messages Get Started

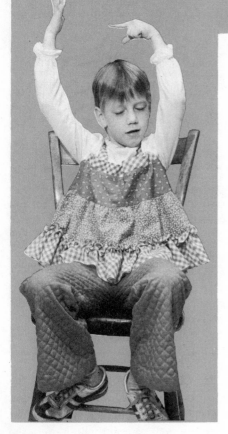

Question:
You have told me how a message is carried by a little nerve fiber in my body. But how do messages get started in the first place?

We have already talked about how a nerve cell or neuron carries a message over its nerve fiber. We were thinking about a nerve fiber connected to a muscle cell. Here the message tells the muscle cell to go to work. Scientists have learned to start a message in the nerve fiber by giving it an electric shock. Of course this is not the way messages usually get started in your body. You want to know how messages usually do get started.

The billions of cells of your nervous system are specialists, each with its own job. There is one kind of cell which has the job of starting messages. It is called a **receptor.** There are many receptor cells in the back of your eye. Each one starts a message when light shines on it. There are receptor cells in your ear which are worked by sound. There are receptor cells on your tongue and in your nose which start messages about taste and smell. And there are receptor cells in your skin which work when the skin is touched, or made hot or cold.

Really we have been thinking about what we call our five senses: sight, hearing, touch, taste, and smell. For each of these senses there are special receptors, or receiving stations, to tell us something about the world around us.

We also have receptors which tell about what is going on inside us. The most interesting of these are the receptors built into our muscles to tell about what our muscles are doing. These have a special name, **proprioceptors** (PRO-pree-oh-SEP-ters).

Since most people don't know about their proprioceptors, let's do an experiment which will show you something about them. Close your eyes. Then slowly wave your left arm around any way you wish. Think about what your arm is doing. How do you know? See if you can touch one finger to your nose. How did you find your nose without watching your hand?

Now let's get both hands into the act. Again, with eyes closed, move your left hand to any position you want and hold it there. Use a finger of your right hand and make it point toward your left hand. Open your eyes and see whether your finger is really pointing toward your left hand.

Maybe you think the experiment was pretty silly. You knew you could do this all the time. But if you think about the experiment, you must ask how you could do it. How do you know what your arms and legs and fingers and toes are doing? Your proprioceptors are always sending in messages to tell what your muscles are doing.

You have many different kinds of receptors or message-starters. Each one is a specialist in the kind of sense it gives. Each receptor cell is connected to the fiber of a nerve cell. This nerve cell or neuron is also a specialist. Its one job is to carry messages from the receptor. The receptors and their connecting neurons are always sending in information about the world around us and about what is happening inside us.

Feedback

The proprioceptors of your muscles serve to give you what engineers call **feedback.** Every time you move a muscle, it sends back messages to tell you how far it has moved. That way you get to correct and smooth out muscle movement.

You can easily place an egg on a plate without breaking it. You slow down your hand as the egg approaches the plate, and the egg makes a safe "soft landing." Space scientists learned that a lot of instruments and carefully controlled machinery are needed to land a spaceship on the moon as softly as you can put an egg on a plate.

The idea of feedback is used in all machinery, such as the thermostat which controls the furnace to keep house temperature constant, and the automatic pilot of ships and planes. But no one has built machines in which feedback works better than it does in control of your body.